Dirt Angels

Donald Platt

New Issues Poetry & Prose

A Green Rose Book

New Issues Poetry & Prose
The College of Arts and Sciences
Western Michigan University
Kalamazoo, Michigan 49008

First Edition, 2009.

ISBN-10   1-930974-82-5 (paperbound)
ISBN-13   978-1-930974-82-1 (paperbound)

Library of Congress Cataloging-in-Publication Data:
Platt, Donald
Dirt Angels/Donald Platt
Library of Congress Control Number: 2008941291

Editor   William Olsen
Managing Editor   Marianne Swierenga
Copy Editor   Kory Shrum
Designer   Danielle Giza
Art Director   Tricia Hennessy
Production Manager   Paul Sizer
                            The Design Center, Frostic School of Art
                            College of Fine Arts
                            Western Michigan University

Dirt Angels

Donald Platt

New Issues

WESTERN MICHIGAN UNIVERSITY

Also by Donald Platt

Fresh Peaches, Fireworks, & Guns
Cloud Atlas
My Father Says Grace

for Eleanor & Lucy

Contents

My Brother's Mirror

At eight years old my brother born with Down syndrome
liked to shuffle
down the sidewalk holding our mother's hand mirror

in which he'd watch
what was happening behind him. What did he see so long ago?
Me on a butterfly-handlebarred

bike, which he would never learn to ride, about to run him down,
shouting, "Look out,
slow poke! Make way, bird brain! Think quick, fat tick!"

I would swerve
around him at the last moment. He gazed back at me with blank
cow eyes and couldn't

speak. He warbled like a sparrow, drooled, and went on
looking
in his mirror. Did he see the wind shake the lilacs

by our neighbor's hedge
back and forth like handbells? They kept ringing out their sweet
invisible scent.

Peals of petals fell to the ground. "Look harder, Michael,"
I want to tell him now.
"Your namesake is an archangel. Do you see Kathy, our beautiful

babysitter, who will
kill herself years later with sleeping pills, waving her white dishtowel
to call us home

to supper?" She once caught me lying on the floor and trying
to look up the dark folds
of her schoolgirl's wool skirt and slapped me. But don't we all

walk forward, gazing backward
over our shoulders at the future coming at us from the past like a hit-and-run
driver? Michael,

God's idiot angel, I see in your mirror our father
                    yanking out
the plugs of all the TVs blaring the evening news

                    on his nursing home's
locked ward for the demented. He hates the noise, the CNN reporters
                    in Bam, Iran,

covering yesterday's earthquake, 6.6 on the Richter scale,
                    twelve seconds,
twenty-five thousand dead, thousands more buried alive

                    beneath the rubble.
The aftershocks continue. We get live footage of a woman in a purple
                    shawl, sifting

through her gold-ringed fingers the crumbled concrete
                    of what were once
the blue-tiled walls of her house. She wails and keeps on

                    digging.
This morning I dreamed that I was building an arch
                    from pieces of charred

brick I'd found in that debris. It was complete except for
                    the keystone,
but no brick would fit. What I needed

                    was our father
to put his splayed fingers into the fresh mortar where the keystone
                    should have gone

and leave his handprints there, so I might put my palms to his.
                    Brother, I held your hand
for the first time last winter. Your fingers were warm,

                    rubbery.
The skin on the back of your hands was rough and chapped.
                    They are the same fingers

that weave placemats from blue wool yarn every day,
                    slowly passing
the shuttle over and under the warp, its strands stretched tight

                    as the strings of a harp.
It's a silent slow music you make. It takes you
                    weeks to weave

a single placemat. Brother, you dropped the hand mirror.
                    It cracked, but didn't
shatter. It broke the seamless sky into countless

                    jagged splinters,
but still holds the aspen's trembling leaves, the lilacs, you and me,
                    all passing things.

First Frost

What flowers are under
that red-and-white-checkered tablecloth, those lavender
bedsheets, that ragged

blue plastic tarpaulin my neighbor has spread
over the low bushes
in her garden to protect them from the first

frost? I think
of how some Catholics still cover the mirrors in their houses
with black veils

after a death. To the mourners the mirrors say, "Yes,
let the world
go dark. Let grief blind you and make you see

how twilight
seeps into the living room even at noon, how the furniture is always shrouded
in shadows so blue

they're black." But the sun is no iron wrecking ball swung
across the sky.
My neighbor has tucked this crazy patchwork around her plants

as a mother might
draw up the blankets that a sick child has kicked off
in restless sleep.

I'm walking our dog through the first frost
that silvers
the grass beneath my feet and in which I leave

dark wet footprints.
The dog runs to each tree in turn and jumps to catch
between her snapping jaws

the squirrels that she smells but cannot see. They scold
and tease her,
trapeze artists of swaying branches. When we arrive

                              back home,
        the sun has melted the hard frost to spangled dew. My neighbor
                              comes out

        in her purple pajamas to check the damage. We wave. She pulls off
                              the garden's slipcovers
        as a magician would the magic cloth he's draped

                              over the empty
        birdcage to reveal not a cooing mourning dove produced
                              from thin air,

        but tall basil, caged tomatoes that are big misshapen fists of jade
                              starting to turn
        red, bell peppers, and a whole gaggle of spindly

                              rust-gold chrysanthemums,
        whose petals are small sunrises. There are other nights and other frosts,
                              stranger sleights of hand to come.

Mid-March at the Park, 2003

                    The first day of spring
after the endless, asphalt-cracking winter and we all go out to the park
                    into the 60-degree

weather to luxuriate in the unfamiliar sun. The young men
                    pull off their shirts
to reveal flabby torsos white as dead fish floating

                    belly-up. Grandparents sit
stunned in the sunlight on park benches carved with initials connected
                    by plus signs. Young mothers

push their toddlers on the creaking swings. Sparrows gossip in the bare bushes.
                    Fathers play
awkward games of catch with their small sons, who invariably

                    miss the ball
and have to run after it over the sodden shag carpet of bleached grass.
                    Dogs leap

to snap frisbees between their teeth. Teenage daughters
                    in skimpy skirts
parade their long, popsicle-stick legs and new breasts

                    the size of unripe
mangoes spilling out of blue tube tops. Their brothers push the smaller
                    kids on the merry-go-round

as fast as they can around the dirt track worn several inches
                    into the ground
by countless feet. They run until they get dizzy and fall down,

                    staining their knees
black with mud. Everyone is waiting for the first purple hearts of crocuses
                    and the war to begin.

Forsythia

Whenever I hear someone say "forsythia," that word
        exploding
into shrapnel petals so abundantly yellow

        it sparks
the spring from black soil and makes the grass catch flame again
        and burn green

under my bare feet, I still hear "for Cynthia." When I was six, its branches
        budded into
a tangle of barbed-wire wildfire for Cynthia,

        my favorite
baby-sitter, whose own lithe trunk had sprouted
        breasts in the last

half year. For her the swallows returned, scissoring
        across the sky's
blue and white finger-painting, cumulus clouds that were

        the wind's palm prints.
For her boys on stingray bicycles swarmed the streets at dusk
        like fireflies

and popped wheelies. The land mines of crocus and daffodil
        detonated
under our feet. Winter's cease-fire was broken. For her it rained

        five days straight.
When the sun came back, our cat Tippy left muddy paw-print
        flowers on the hot hood

of our white Chevy, the engine still ticking after the ignition
        had been turned off.
For her Ralph, the scrawny neighbor kid, climbed onto his wet

        roof on Easter Sunday and threw
raw eggs at us. One splattered against the ripe swell of her hip. Its yolk
        dripped yellow down

her blue denim dress and onto her bare calf's winter-white
                    skin. For her
I yelled, shook my fists at him, and dared him

                    to come down
and be a man. She only laughed, blew him a kiss, dipped her index finger
                    into the yolk

and streaked my nose yellow. Forsythia. For Cynthia.
                    Let all our words
cross-pollinate, misspoken and misheard.

Girls with Glow-in-the-Dark Hula Hoops

The black girl
        Labetta from the next house over
                is teaching my daughter Eleanor

to do the hula hoop, to shake her hips
        in that rhythmical
                unmistakably sexual

shimmy, though they are still
        saplings, birch
                and ash growing together

on the same boiling
        hopscotch-chalked street.
                And though I feel the long

kiss of history
        as I breathe in the Georgia dusk's
                humid pine odor

and see within the lilac's sweet shadows
        the slave ghosts hoe rock and red clay
                and shuffle in their musical

cruel shackles toward the auction
        block in Charleston,
                which is now a tourist attraction,

my daughter and her friend don't
        yet feel the ironies radiate
                like the day's heat

up from the asphalt
        through the soles of their matching
                pink sneakers. As they grow

into their bodies and fill out
        the hourglass shapes that spell
                women, so they

must grow into history and put on
            guilt's glitter, anger's
                        lipstick and sequins.

But now they are only
            two girls out late
                        after dinner, alone with the slow sparks

of fireflies in the dusk that gathers
            and deepens into
                        night, that takes them

into her arms like an anonymous
            mother and makes them over
                        until I can't tell

one body from
            the other. And now, because I am
                        nearsighted, there are only two

hula hoops, glowing
            yellow-green, revolving as if
                        by themselves, haloes around

the invisible place where
            their bodies were, night's lost
                        daughters found, who wear in their

dark hair
            fireflies, in their earlobes
                        the seed-pearl stars.

Loose Change & Molars

Because I don't want
Lucy at seven years old to know that I am the tooth fairy,
I turn away

from her when I empty the coin purse into my palm
to scrounge
enough money to buy her an ice cream

cone with jimmies.
I hold in my hand the silver and copper coins and four
of her teeth—

two molars, an incisor, and a canine—that I couldn't bring
myself to throw
away, but put in my purse for safekeeping on those nights

I tiptoed into
her room, reached under the pillow, chanted my abracadabras,
and changed her teeth

to cold cash. Now, counting out my last dimes
and nickels,
I wonder how much these four teeth will buy. Shall I open

in her name a bank account
with them as my initial deposit, or use them as the down payment
on a house

that's not yet built? Her small tongue wiggled them
loose. They ached
to their roots. Like Eve, she bit into a green apple, and they fell

out. One day
they and their secret pain will be all that's left of her childhood, and I will
count them over

and over, millionaire of these hours compounded daily.
She smiles
her gappy smile. I have enough change to buy her

a mocha chip
double-dip with rainbow jimmies in a sugar cone. She curves
her pink tongue

around its scooped, sculpted coolness. "Do you want a lick?"
"Sure," I say.
I taste the cold sweetness of our long summer days together.

The loose change
and teeth rattle in my coin purse like the wildflower seeds
in their paper packet,

which my daughter and I broadcast across our backyard.
Shall I plant her molars
in the black soil? By the time they flower, my daughter will be grown and gone.

Provider

for Tom Andrews, 1961-2001

Your life is the caked
black dirt beneath my fingernails that I can't yet bear to wash
off. I struggle

to extricate the fuzzy, red-tinged stems and serrated
leaves of the strawberries
from the nettles, dandelions, wild parsley, and crab grass that have grown

around them. The root
systems of weed and fruit are so intertwined I have to separate them
from each other

with a safecracker's touch, and often the strawberries
get pulled up
with the weeds and have to be thrown onto

the same pile.
It's useless to explain a death like yours.
You died

too young. Your early poems emerged full-formed
and sweet to taste
as the knuckle-sized strawberries two months ago, on which

I gorged
and gorged red-mouthed. I prune the strawberries back
so they will come

again next year. Now, on the day before
my own
forty-fourth birthday, I pick the first

green beans
of the season. They hide beneath the large, veined,
heart-shaped leaves,

which still bear small purple flowers. Dana, my wife, says
        this particular variety
is called "Provider." I snap off one of the young

        beans thin as shoelaces.
Nothing's more tender. We eat them raw. They are crisp with juice.
        Along with the sweet

dissolving fiber, there are always a few grains of the dirt's
        grit. Tom, I wish
you too might taste it. It's like eating water.

Elegy in Spring Snow

April 8th, a freak snow five days after Easter,
          and the daffodils,
which had opened their mouths and shouted yellow

          yellow against
the sodden mass of brown and purplish dead leaves
          in our backyard,

are now six inches under. The white melting shroud flashes
          a whiplash of lightning
in the sun and makes my eyes wince shut and squint.

          Everyone leaves
shining footprints that by tomorrow will turn to muddy water
          gargling down

the storm drain. I can't stop thinking of the way the curly-haired
          checkout boy
at Evergood Grocery shook each paper bag open with a quick, insouciant

          flick of the wrist,
made the creased paper crack like a slapshot off the rink's boards,
          and then packed the bag full,

canned goods and milk at the bottom, eggs and big heads
          of frilly escarole
on top. Today I heard the cashier tell how last night

          the boy's souped-up
Camaro had skidded on a slick S-curve as he came into
          work in the falling

snow. He hit a concrete pylon head-on. His neck
          broke. I'm thinking
of the blond daffodils packed tight in snow's

          excelsior, some
with their green stems snapped, others that will survive
          the storm. Who

decides what lives or dies? What is this gift we get, snow
                that blossoms and loads
the bare pear trees, then bends their branches to the ground? They don't

                spring back. Tomorrow, when we set
our clocks forward, lose an hour, it won't matter to the boy who has forgotten
                daylight and how to save it.

After the Death of the Poet

for Donald Justice, 1925-2004

It is as if
he is still playing the piano in the next room—something baroque,
            maybe a Bach toccata,

or some improvisation on diminished chords by Mingus or Monk.
            Sometimes it sounds
like loquacious rain on an overturned iron washtub. At others, a crazed

            cadenza for two
woodpeckers tapping out morse code along the taut electric nerves
            of tree trunks. But no,

when I open the door, the room is empty. I run my fingers
            over the intricate
scrollwork of lacquered teak against which the sheet music

            once leaned.
It holds nothing now. On the closed soundboard he has left
            the small black pyramid

of his metronome ticking adagio, our common measure, sixty-five
            heartbeats per minute.
Dead poet, what music vibrates and spirals

            along the delicate
cochlea of your inner ear, those notes you still transmute,
            transmit

through invisible fingertips to black or white keys that make
            felt hammers
strike the dumbstruck strings inside us all?

Human Poem

Reading Vallejo's *Poemas Humanos* for the first time, a bilingual
        edition (how foolish
never to have learned Spanish . . .), I find a postcard stuck in the middle

        as a bookmark.
It shows three white birches with their heart-shaped, serrated leaves
        through which the camera gazes

out over a lake on whose waves the sunlight lies hammered
        to thin gold foil
and, beyond the lake, mountains blue-green in the haze of midsummer.

        I turn the card over.
It is addressed to "Dear Danacita" from her friend Valerie—"Oh Joy! Sunshine,
        cows, and crackling

fires at night. Love all over the place. Yum . . ." Val's husband,
        Jim, has added
a postscript—"Yah! Whoooa! Some fun!" I look

        at the postmark—
fourteen years ago, the summer they were married. So this must have been
        their honeymoon,

Harvey's Lake, West Barnet, Vermont. It's Dana's paperback
        so she was probably
reading this page when the postcard arrived with its wild

        scrawl sloping
upwards to the right with happiness. I read Vallejo's lines
        at the top of the left

page aloud in my halting Italian-accented Spanish, "De disturbio en disturbio
        subes a acompañarme
a estar solo," and then look to the right-hand translation for help:

        "From disturbance
to disturbance you rise to accompany me to be alone."
        Val hardly

writes us anymore. They're still married, though for six months
                    she lived in Arizona
with another man. From disturbance to disturbance, Dana

                    and I also walk.
How did Vallejo know? *To accompany me to be alone.*
                    Last night Dana sobbing

into her pillow at 3:38 A.M. by the glowing hands
                    of my alarm clock,
and I in another bed, pretending to be asleep and not to hear.

The Breakage

Finally his wife tells him that every day for the last three years
        she has been thinking of leaving
him. Mostly she doesn't say anything, though once when his awkward

        arm brushed to the ground
a matching cut-glass decanter and sugar bowl, things that held nothing
        but refracted the light

and threw it in random rainbows around the room,
        she yelled
for hours. Mostly she remains silent, but he

        catches her
looking at him as if she doesn't recognize him, as if
        he's a stranger

who happens to be standing next to her in a crowded bus terminal,
        as they both wait in line
to buy a ticket out. He tells himself that she "suffers" him,

        and he finds himself
treating her gently, formally, even after they make love, brushing the hair
        out of her eyes

for her with one thumb before leaving the bed in which he doesn't
        sleep anymore.
Their two daughters watch them walk through

        the maze of their intricate
days in zigzags that occasionally intersect. He wonders what
        his daughters will remember

of these costly silences in their double-mortgaged house
        with its huge
skylights that fill the living room with wall-to-wall sunlight.

        Last summer
his younger daughter found four rocks in the garden,
        washed them off,

painted green stems with rosebuds on each, and named them
                      Mama Rock,
Papa Rock, Sister Rock, and Baby Rock. A family of stones about to flower.

                 What he will remember
is how every night for the last ten years he has bathed
               one or the other

of his two daughters, slid the soap along their smooth, tanned
                limbs, lathered
their hair into eighteenth-century wigs, and poured water

               over their streaming
heads with "bailers," plastic pint containers that once held choice oysters.
               "Do you know

how I know I'm growing?" his younger daughter asked him
               yesterday. "See how
I'm longer than the bathtub now? Soon I won't fit in it anymore

               and will be able
only to take showers." He toweled roughly her wet blond hair.
               This is what he stands to lose.

Dirt Angels

Because there is no snow
in south Georgia at Christmas, my two daughters go out
to lie in the red clay

and make dirt angels. They beat their arms
in the cold dust
like the wings of hurt birds trying to lift off

from this earth.
Though they must return to the voice of their mother shrieking
them home, to the silences

of their father, which fill the house like early winter
twilight, they leave
in the bare spots of the front yard these barely perceptible

fossils of themselves that will
vanish under the stampede of tomorrow's oblivious footprints.
I go out to walk

the dog in the half-light of first morning. There has been a hard
frost, and the ground shines
as if it were not rutted soil, frozen dogshit, and dead grass

but some unspoiled
radiance. The dog sniffs the dirt angels and whines because she knows
they are alive.

If the dirt angels suddenly rise from the shallow graves
where they have lain
dreaming of flying all night and clap their clay wings about

my thick head and stammer
in childhood's trebles, what unpronounceable words would they give
me? I think they would say,

"Return to your daughters, go back to your wife. Tell them
you'll change the way you live."
Fathers have no wings. Love is the hard ground where I must walk

on my knees and eat
the red clay, savor the indigestible grit of the world, open
my mouth, and speak

words that are black mud. "Praise the dirt," the angels shout, and then
they are gone.
The dog barks. Where am I? What am I doing

standing stiller than stone
in a small yard on our dead-end street? The dog pulls the choke chain
to tell me it's time to move on.

Child Sleeping

My six-year-old daughter can fall asleep anywhere in this broad world.
        Tonight it's a noisy
Greek restaurant in downtown Chicago, and there amid

        tyropitakia, dolmatos,
avgolemono soup, calamari, bowls of black olives and feta, her head wobbles
        on its stalk, and she

can eat no more. So we spread her long limbs out on three
        spindly wooden chairs,
and within seconds she is dreaming. My wife points to

        her lips, which pucker
together, relax, pucker over and over. "See, she's nursing. She nursed
        for three and a half years,

and, even though she doesn't remember it, her mouth does!"
        My wife smiles
to herself and then turns to Eleanor, "Oh, I have been blessed

        with two beautiful
daughters . . ." Eleanor switches seats with me so she too can see
        her sister's mouth working

the swollen breast, waiting for the thin air to let down and spurt
        warm milk
against the back of her throat. Lucy can't swallow fast enough

        and her mouth all
but overflows. She gargles in her dream. Nothing will wake her.
        I pay the bill,

scoop Lucy up, and let Dana fit those small floppy arms into the sleeves
        of her too-large
hand-me-down coat. I carry her down North Halsted St. past the young

        childless couples
making out in shadowed doorways, past the old snarling drunk
        with the paper bagged

bottle clenched between his shaking knees, past police sirens and the epileptic
        seizures of their flashing
lights, past the gold rope chains and black leather of the hustlers, past the frat boy

        dry-heaving on his knees
in the gutter. Nothing wakes her. It is a 50-degree Saturday night in early
        March, and everybody

is out walking the streets. The crowd parts for me. Lucy's breathing
        is even and sure. The air
smells of grilled sausage. She grows heavier, so I stop to adjust

        her loose weight cradled
against my chest. All I can see now of her head hidden deep in her coat's hood
        is the scroll

of one pink ear that hears yells, curses, and tires screeching as a car pulls out
        from the curb—
still asleep, she is not disturbed. A man stops his long black Buick

        in the middle of traffic,
opens his door and shouts out to us, "Do you need a ride? Where are you going?"
        I tell him it's OK,

our run-down hotel is two blocks away. He nods, reassured.
        Only then do I see
how I've been carrying life itself in weak arms down a one-way street.

Spring Theophanies

The pear trees
put on their white see-through chemise of blossoms
that the season will strip

from them until they stand shy, shivering with rain,
and green. Someone
has toilet-papered the apple tree in my neighbor's

front yard. Slow burn
of redbud, and two street preachers come out
and shout salvation

through megaphones to the pigeons, to the traffic jam
of cars idling and throbbing
with rap, their basses wah-wahing, and hold up

cue cards for the stammering
soul: "Thus Saith the Lord of Hosts, Consider Your Ways."
Consider Madam Bell,

late-night TV psychic, found floating facedown
in a reflecting pool,
who drowned without foretelling her own

end and left
on the park bench her handbag stuffed with cash and checks
for deposit only

beside her neatly folded white socks and polished penny loafers.
Consider the all-night
laundromats where a few tennis shoes orbit endlessly in the dark

of the dryers on the permanent
press cycle. Consider also the day lilies that rage in the drainage ditches
for a week or two and are gone

as if they had never been. Read your fortune in the many empty palms
the world holds out to you
on West Peachtree Street. Give them whatever you can

                    spare—loose change,
paper clips, a comb missing some of its teeth, your tangled rosary,
                    the phone number

of the woman with pink-streaked hair, whom you wanted so badly
                    to kiss, but didn't,
or the opening seven words of a poem you'll probably never

                    get around to writing,
scribbled on the cover of a matchbook. Strike. Ignite. Let all our inflammable syllables
                    go up and burn down

to the ground, the cracks in the sidewalk where the crab grass keeps
                    growing. Nothing
will salvage us, only ravage us. So where

                    does God dwell
if not with the homeless? If not with the wasps that I evict
                    with a burning, gasoline-soaked

rag on the end of a stick? If not with the fire ants
                    whose high rises
I raze with my riding lawn mower, suburban

                    engine of revenge?
I am their whirlwind and terrorism. Consider your ways, says the Lord.
                    Consider, too, the convicts

who, now that spring is here, pick up the winter's litter on the shoulders
                    of the road. They come
to us in school buses painted white and are dressed in white with a single

                    line of blue piping
down the sides of their trousers. Are they our holy ones, seraphim in disguise?
                    No untouchable angels, they

have fallen and been sentenced for several consecutive lifetimes
        to harvest the trash
from our freeways. A few have been condemned to lay down new blacktop

        in our neighborhood.
They have chosen the fattest convict, at least four hundred heavenly, unleavened
        pounds, to ride

the steamroller. Consider how it crushes everything
        to black
glitter, and makes smooth and straight

        the way of the Lord.
Hot odor of tar mingles with honeysuckle and fresh, fly-bejeweled
        dog turd. The kids can't resist

the asphalt's black velvet. They go out and scribble lopsided hearts,
        stick figures
of their ponytailed selves, and giant peonies of suns

        risen from the night's road
paved by men doing time, amen, for their petty and violent sins. Breaking
        and entering, rape,

rage, double homicide are always here beneath the street
        we walk the dog down
every morning. The children, when their imagination

        fails them as it must,
do not put down their chalk, but draw their own houses,
        larger than "life-size"

blueprints, empty quarter-block-long rectangles
        for each floor connected
by zigzags that mean stairs, and then start filling in

        everything that surrounds
us, the pots, pans, TVs, tables, armchairs, stoves with small crowns of fire
        a child might wear, everything that is

and is not our lives. If they would listen, I'd tell them not to stop,
                but dusk comes,
mothers call them home, and one day soon April's

                torrential rains will wash
their half-finished, halfway houses back to flat, black street. Consider all
                those colors.

Elegy in the Rainbow Season

I had forgotten
that West Virginia is coal country. I woke up
in a Days Inn, south

of Charleston, and while my wife and two kids slept
I went down and walked
the riprap of the riverbank to watch the barges loaded with black

glinting coal
churn down the Kanawha River, pushing pillows of water
before them

and leaving behind them brief white wakes, a V of waves
that turned
to lisping ripples on the stones at my feet. And then I remembered

that this was the country
not only of coal, hidden in its deep underground seams, but of my dead friend,
the poet Tom Andrews,

who had been born just north of here and had died on another continent
eleven months ago.
What was there left to say, stammer out, or sing? Did he know this slow

bend of the river
spanned by a rusted iron bridge painted primer gray
or the Show Bar

& Cheetah Lounge, one hundred yards upstream, now only charred joists
black against fuchsia
clapboards, all stitched together with the tendrils of morning glories?

Without warning it started
to rain, a warm windless spring rain that fell perpendicular to the ground.
What did it matter that I got

soaked to the skin? I muttered one last prayer for Tom. Hail Mary,
full of grace. Hail
the coal barges of the dead, sunk low in the water with their load,

                    hail black lung
which each miner tunnels toward, hail the green-shag-carpeted
                    mountains worn bare

by strip mines . . . Then it stopped raining as suddenly
                    as it had started.
The sun burned through. Ghosts of steam rose from the asphalt.

                    I walked back
across the parking lot and looked up and saw part of a rainbow
                    whose curve described

the same arc as that of the iron bridge, which joined the two sides of the river,
                    run-down shotgun bungalows
on the east bank, wide-verandaed Victorians on the west. I saw

                    the fresh puddles scummed
with oil slick that for a moment became a fire-eater's mouth breathing out
                    tongues of flame,

which then turned back to oil slick. The rainbow had disappeared.
                    A carrot-haired woman
in bell-bottom blue jeans walked barefoot across the rainbowed puddles.

                    She didn't see me,
stretched out both hands, palms upturned, as if she could hold at once
                    the sunlight and the rain.

Sentence Fragment Ending in Sleep's Ellipsis

My other life, the one that comes to me after we make love,
        our two middle-aged bodies
like old unused doors sighing open and shut, revealing an unfurnished

        room, where the sunlight
through the window makes on the floorboards a white prayer mat
        where I would

kneel, bow down, and chant the psalm of your damp skin against
        mine, our limbs
curved around each other like two dark tangled eyelashes

        of a single eye
that has gazed straight at the sun's golden, die-stamped coin
        and now closes

as we enter the slow dissolve of two bodies falling
        asleep
together . . . we are snow drifting down

        on a blossoming
apple tree in late April so it's impossible to tell
        snowflake from petal . . .

What Form Shall the Soul Take?

I put both palms
into the concrete handprints on the top step of our stoop
above the name

Marian Hensler, 1989, and my hands, fingers splayed wide,
fit her hands
exactly. Through the cold concrete scrabbly as coarse-grit

sandpaper, I am
palm to palm with someone I will never meet,
but my hands understand

what she must have felt beneath the mazed whorls of her own fingertips.
Hot water sluicing
from the faucet, splashing into the bath. Cat's scratch. Slubbed silk.

Flat oval stone held
between thumb and index finger, cocked back by the wrist, and then flicked
to skip over

the lake's surface, a scared animal's heartbeat—she counts four skittery
jumps before it goes
under. Her lover's aroused nipples like the thumb-polished beads

of a rosary
she says every morning. The warm, twice-risen, sourdough loaves
she kneads her anger into

after her mother died without warning. The worn glass doorknob
of the hollow-core
door she has opened and left ajar so that the flawed music

from the old
upright, some minuet by Bach, may travel from room to empty
room. The static

electric shock as she reaches out to pet the cat's winter coat.
O Marian Hensler,
O 1989, year my wife got pregnant with our firstborn, will the ten thousand

living things we touch every day
turn only to two cold handprints in concrete? Will we become
no more

than an old woman, washing her ragged underwear by hand
each evening
in a chipped porcelain sink, stained the colors of sunset

where the iron beneath
the enamel has rusted through, who whispers to herself, "Poor soul, poor soul"
like the whippoorwill?

No, the soul is billion and gold bullion. It lives in the wet
concrete that takes
the starred imprint of a woman's palm and hardens.

Bloodstone

I wear a dead man's bloodstone cufflinks.
        They are the amber
of beads of resin bleeding from a gash in a pine

        and hardened. Set
in old 14-karat gold, they once belonged to Crepps,
        my wife's step-grandmother's

brother, who died at twenty-four in the year
        panic slashed and burned
the stock market. That's almost all I know of him. Hearsay

        has it that he "lived
hard," which back then, in Kentucky, meant bourbon, horses, and women.
        "Crepps"—was it a nickname

or some favorite great-aunt's last name plucked from a dead
        branch of the family
tree and grafted onto his new flesh to bear

        more fruit? What fruit
but early death's wild quince blossom? Holding the cufflinks
        in my palm, I rub them

with a thumb to feel their worn smoothness. Did he
        hold them so?
They are the one thing that connects us. No life

        is ever entirely
lost. I inhale the dark smell of whiskey on his breath, the gardenias
        he plucked for his girl

and set in a tumbler of water, those two perfumes that fill my own room
        tonight. What better elegy?
His name alive in my mouth, the burn of whiskey, two cufflinks made of bloodstone.

Spring Does Covers & Original Numbers

Spring is the 24-hour-a-day
jam session of the dead who live in the basement apartment
next door. We never

see them go out for groceries or lunch dates. Their notes
rise from
the ground. Those daffodils are the blare of Miles Davis's

dented
unmutable trumpet. Of course, the crocuses are Thelonius Monk
improvising

some bright melody on only the black keys. Billie Holiday
sings through the bruised
throats of the irises. Ella's in the azaleas. Coltrane hums

"A Love Supreme"
among the honeysuckle. "We're back!" yell the perennials.
"Did you think

we'd left you?" joke the dead. "We love your cooking too much,
Big Daddy.
Your first spring barbecues are our burnt offerings. Give us

bourbon and spareribs
glazed with brown sugar and hot sauce, and we'll play for you always.
Man, you got to dig

death. Our voices get transposed into a silent
key. We're better
than forever. We do all the old covers and original numbers."

That riff of red
tulips on the corner of 10th and Vine St. is Art Blakey taking
a fifteen-minute

drum solo. The poppies on Schuyler Avenue with their orange
organdy skirts,
which my wife covets, sway in time to Benny Goodman's

clairvoyant
clarinet. The blowsy peonies planted in whitewall tires
                along the back alley

are Louis Armstrong's sweat-stained silk handkerchiefs
                after recording
all night live at Basin St. My favorite number's still the shush of wind

                in the fitful
maple leaves and the scat of early morning's scattered birdsong. "Any
                last requests?"

growls Louis. "Yes," I tell him, "play 'Wisteria!'" And now
                Satchmo's notes
grow lavender cone-shaped clusters of spit-curl petals

                which hang heavy
as ripe grapes on vines that spell out his sinuous signature
                tune. I catch

their raw perfume on the air. Spring is continual
                orgasm.
The dead mainline the heroin of memory and desire. They're cooking.

                Charlie Parker's bebop
on alto sax twirls down like the thousands of helicopter seeds
                from the maples, which clog

our gutters that spill over during the next hard rain in a musical
                waterfall.
I watch a robin pull a long naked worm from the drowned ground

                and devour it
whole. What's it like to be a half note in that insatiable throat? "It's cramped
                down here," say the dead.

"Don't mess with us. We've got some more chord changes to work out now."
                They're playing their slide
trombones. The tall violet columbines keep coming into bloom.

Jumping the Waves

Nothing else exists
for her but the sun and the flint glint of these waves crashing over us, inexorable
tons of slate-blue

salt water that crests with the delicacy of a fantail pigeon spreading
its ruff of white
feathers, then smashes load upon load of loud crockery,

a dump truck
emptying an avalanche of shining hissing debris around our knees.
I hold my daughter Lucy

under the armpits and feel her heart jar and startle
beneath the rungs
of her ribs, wing-beats of a pheasant flushed

from its thicket
by far-off gunshot. She arches her back, as I lift her over each exploding comber.
Her taut body trembles

with high voltage, conductor through which all things flow. She swallows sea water,
laughs, and reaches both hands
to the breakers whose undertow nearly knocks me flat. "Mama, come closer,"

she screams over
and over. "Mama, make me another wave. Mama,
I love you." The ocean

obliges. Its rise and fall is that of a great patient beast
breathing. I see again
the mother mallard leading her string of seven green and yellow

ducklings into this morning's
four lanes of rush-hour traffic. I skidded to a stop. The car next to me
swerved and clipped

the seventh duckling's tail-feathers. But it got up and kept waddling after
its mother. They all
crossed the highway only inches from our fenders while we gawked. My daughter

strains forward for the next
wave, for delight, for what will catch her up and tumble her
under the surf with the stones

and smashed beach glass that the ocean's molars grind down
to the sweet smoothness
of half-sucked lozenges. Her body is a bow bent

with an arrow that I hold back
for only this flexed second and then must let go and watch fly beyond the breakers
toward the blind sun's bull's-eye.

Winter Water

When I see my father's slack,
loose-fleshed face, stained with liver spots, crosshatched with broken blood
        vessels, I think

of John Keats's life mask, its hollowed cheeks, and how he must have had
        to hold still
while the plaster cast dried against his new-shaven

        skin and he breathed in
and out through straws inserted into his nostrils. Is that what dying
        is like, to feel

quarter-inch-thick plaster harden over your face so you can't
        smile, wince, speak
anymore? "I can scarcely bid you good bye

        even in a letter,"
Keats wrote to Charles Brown. "I always made
        an awkward bow."

I bow down before my father and touch his wooden
        face, last night's
dream totem. We must leave each other soon. When I look

        into his shallow
blurred eyes, I see only the gray winter pools of abandoned marble quarries.
        I remember standing

on snow-covered ground, at the silent lip of that water,
        and looking down.
Nothing looked back or spoke. But if I threw chunks of bread

        that I had torn
from the stale loaf I carried with me always and had rolled into smooth
        balls between my fingers,

I would see in that slate-gray water the flicker of flames
        smoldering below
the still surface. It was like blowing on almost dead coals. Suddenly

the red-gold
giant carp would rise, strike that bait, swallow the bread, and then sink back,
fed, to where they had come from.

En Passant

My father takes his dying
slow. "Why should I get out of bed anymore?" he asks
his nurses. They roll

him over like a great beached sperm whale so he won't get
bedsores.
Because his lungs have become congested,

every morning
for ten minutes they put him on a breathing machine,
which breathes back

medicinal mist into the vacuum bags of his lungs
tired of sucking
in, out, in, out. Father, do you remember

teaching me
to play chess? You showed me how to capture a pawn
en passant. Your lightning

attacks routed my men. Now, on your good days, you take half an hour
to make each move
and must ask my daughter, "Which side is mine?" Eleanor replies,

"Grandfather, yours
are the white pieces." Yesterday morning, when she asked your long-dead
brother's name, you smiled

ruefully and said, "That doesn't ring any bells with me. But then again
I don't have many
bells to ring." We couldn't help laughing. A nurse comes to check

your blood pressure.
Death will take you *en passant*, when we least expect it,
moving diagonally

from one column to another, white square to white
square, side-stepping
behind you, silent black pawn. *En passant*

meaning "in passing"
or "by the way." Why have our lives been only
this casual conversation

between two distant acquaintances, who stop on the street to exchange
pleasantries about
tornado warnings, then say goodbye, and pass on

to their next
errand? Is there no final colloquy, no grand finale to be performed
between us?

Late afternoons you grow marvelously incoherent.
You tell me, "I'm sure
we can come to some understanding. But where are the people

who represent
the beach, the trees, the party favors?" I don't know how
to answer. We watch

snow flurries swirl furiously in the dusk outside your window.
We are cut-glass
figures of passersby in a cut-glass town submerged

in the waters
of a glass globe, which a bored child shakes
and shakes to see

the snow, confetti that has settled
to the ground,
fly up again, whirl and eddy.

End Game

My father and I play our last game of chess in Budapest

*

We play at a sidewalk café under an orange-and-blue-striped umbrella

*

It is dusk, we drink Campari mixed with Perrier and lime

*

Both of my father's castles are missing

*

In their place he puts small piles of green seaweed salad and moves them around the
board with chopsticks

*

A few small boys come over to our table to watch the game

*

My father slides his black bishop forward, it turns into a clump of steamed white rice

*

He eats it

*

My father takes my pawn with his knight and the pawn becomes a flapping minnow

*

He smiles, catches the minnow in his cupped hands, puts it in his water glass, and
drinks

*

His hairy Adam's apple bobs as he swallows

*

The minnow swims in small frantic circles inside the glass

*

The waiter walks over to watch

*

I castle, and my rook changes into a fire-bellied toad, which jumps off the board and is
        chased down the cobblestone street by the small boys who hop after it and croak

*

My father, who has never smoked in his life, lights up a Gauloise and blows smoke
        rings at the full moon as it rises

*

I capture my father's knight, and it turns into a ballerina pirouetting on top of a music
        box, which plays "The Blue Danube"

*

The waiter gets bored and walks away

*

My father stamps on the music box until it splinters

*

The splinters keep playing "The Blue Danube"

*

"Goddamn," mutters my father, "I told your mother never to cook coquilles St. Jacques again—she knows how I hate the smell of scallops!"

*

I tell my father not to indulge in non sequiturs

*

My father takes my queen, which becomes a raw oyster on a half shell

*

My father tastes it

*

He spits it out

*

"They're trying to poison me!" he yells. "Where's the chef?"

*

Only three pieces remain on the board—my king, his king and queen

*

"This is checkmate," he says

*

He moves his queen, which turns into a speckled pebble

*

I move my king, it becomes water

*

He moves his king, which changes to ash

*

This is the game we never finish

Grout

What I remember best
of that year was the graffiti written on the grouting between the gray-flecked
inch-square tiles

of a men's room on the third floor of the university library
where I studied
for doctoral exams. Hundreds of different hands had printed

in the crevices
with minuscule letters an ode to grout: TWIST &
GROUT / BIRDS

FLY GROUT IN THE WINTER / SUCK MY HARD GROUT / EAR, NOSE,
& GROUT / GROUTCHO
MARX / GENGHIS GROUT / LIVE FREE OR GROUT / GRILLED

GROUT AMANDINE /
GREAT GROUT ALMIGHTY / EXISTENTIAL GROUT /
I GROUT

THEREFORE I AM. Reading that too clever graffiti, I thought
inexplicably
of human history, which is like watching late-night TV, some psycho

psychic on a reality show
foretelling the next suicide bomber in Iraq, endless infomercials about penile
enlargement, reruns

of Most Spectacular NASCAR Crashes, cars on fire
pirouetting, then body-slamming
into concrete walls, the driver walking away from it all and waving

to his drunk fans
before the wreckage explodes, or live indoor rodeos where men in leather chaps
try to hang on

to plunging, careening, breakdancing bulls for the eternity
of eight short
seconds, one hand on the hemp cinch, the other flying loose

and flapping
like some spastic's arm in a grand mal seizure. THREE STRIKES & YOU'RE
        GROUT! / ALL YOU NEED

IS GROUT . . . Those bad puns spread like the black plague
        until the whole
wall was an epidemic, a huge crossword of vertical

        and horizontal
phrases in the cracks, a gridwork of words that the janitor didn't
        scrub off, but kept

reading, marveling at the inspired silliness of the human
        mind, when greatly
bored. . . . GROUT, GROUT, BRIEF CANDLE / GROUTICIDE /

        GROUTITUDE /
GROUT AT THE END OF THE RAINBOW / GROUTOGRAPHERS
        OF THE WORLD,

UNITE! / THE GROUT, IT WILL WITHER AWAY / SHUT YOUR
        GROUT . . .
The bathroom wall was a loud lexicon of the one indivisible

        word that held
the tiles together, that would be erased, then rewritten, a clamor
        of tongues, grout's

graffiti scrawled and spelled out on the grouting. All day I had studied
        until my eyes were sore
that epic of rage and killing in which Achilles

        butchered Hector
and promised the dying man to feed his body
        to the dogs, then dragged

the corpse, stabbed at least eighty times by the Achaeans
        and attached by a towrope
to the gilded chariot, while he whipped his geldings over the ruts.

I read how Hector's wife
had prepared a cauldron of hot water for her husband to bathe in
and wash the dirt

of battle from his smooth, shining skin. Then she heard
Hecuba, his mother,
keening and foreknew the slaughter. To rest my eyes

I kept reading
that graffiti. BLOOD, SWEAT, & GROUT / CROPS FAILED
IN THE GROUT /

HOOF & GROUT DISEASE / SAUERGROUTEN. I considered my own
self-destructive
behaviors: how, high on Sherman sticks—marijuana spliffs

soaked in embalming
fluid—I once did the hula dance on a railroad
trestle and mooned

the oncoming freight train, then hung by my knees from a crosstie
while the freight cars
thundered and shuddered two feet above me. The clangor

of those steel wheels,
the rails groaning out GROUT GROUT, shook me to my bones, bruised
and rearranged my inner organs

until I became the tongue of a bronze bell swung wildly back and forth
by unseen
bell-ringers. I went back to Homer's hexameters and read

how Priam
embraced the knees of his son's killer and how Achilles the bully
wept. I looked out

the library window at the construction site four stories below
where men in yellow
hard hats were pouring foundations, the concrete taking the shape of the plywood

forms, their splintered
wood's cirrus grain, its knots and whorls, impressed there like fossils.
One man knelt in the mud,

vomiting. Did he have a fever? Hangover? He retched and retched until nothing
more came up.
Finally, he stood and walked shakily back to work. All I could do was watch.

Consolation Baptist Church

Console me, O Lord,
for I have been driving again the back roads of your promised land,
            past Temple, Georgia

and Mt. Zion, where the red clay has been soaked and washed
            in the blood
of the slaughtered Lamb and still shows its fresh stain. Out of this ground

            come your congregations,
Church of God of Prophecy, Just Endtime Revival Ministries, Full Gospel Choir,
            Joy of the Lord

Deliverance Tabernacle, and Pleasant Grove Baptist. Out of our red clay
            come sweet-smelling
pines with bark scaly as the backs of alligators, and the Speedy Spot

            convenience store
where you can pump your own gas and buy Mayfield milk
            at the same low price

per gallon. The people of my land have tied yellow bows
            with yellow ribbon
around the rusted mailboxes at the ends of their short dirt drives to celebrate

            the defeat of Saddam Hussein
by their sons and daughters in Iraq's deserts. This morning I passed a sign
            that said, "Let's Kick

Some Sand, Nigger Ass" next to "Doughnuts and Fried Pies."
            Sweet Jesus,
why is hate the daily bread we eat? Why do half

            the farmhouses
fly the Stars and Bars over fields where cows graze the dew-soaked
            starry grass?

When I opened my car door in the Piggly Wiggly parking lot
            to buy
spring water last night, a white man in tan overalls

with a three-day growth
of straw-stubble beard shook my hand and said, "Let me witness
to you, good brother!"

Lord, forgive me. I told him I was a Catholic, which in these parts
is two rungs above
being black. He flinched. I walked away. Holy Mary,

virgin mother of God,
let me witness to the roadsides of west Georgia, where day lilies bloom
with their pure orange flames

among the litter of beer cans, paper bags full of cold
congealed French fries,
and crumpled crotch shots of centerfolds from *Hustler* or *Stroke*

thrown out the open windows
of pickup trucks at 2 A.M., eighty miles per hour. Flowers and litter
are equally anointed

by morning's heavy dew. Let me count again the freight cars
of the Norfolk Southern
slowly crossing Hog Liver Rd. with their steel wheels grinding

and ringing against
the rails, while I wait in my car for the train to pass, couplings
clanging on the downgrade,

and see the graffiti on their sides, swirls and broken arcs
of spray-painted
rainbow letters elaborate as the Book of Kells, FAT BOY,

JASPAR,
and FUCK ALL HONKIES. Let me not forget the beautiful, expressionless
face of the black

woman at the DQ's drive-thru as she handed me my soft-serve
vanilla cone,
our hands brushing against each other briefly like the wings of shy birds

as we passed
money back and forth. I will always remember the riddle and its answer
                scrawled in black permanent marker

on the gas station's smut-glutted urinal wall—WHY IS AN APPLE
                LIKE A NIGGER?
GOD MEANT FOR THEM BOTH TO HANG FROM TREES.

                Father, how
can you forgive us? In one of the stained-glass windows of Consolation
                Baptist Church,

where I have come at noon to get out of the heat,
                Thomas puts
his fingers into Christ's raw flayed side. There is no

                other way. *Put
your hands into each of my wounds*, the harsh light streaming
                through the window

commands. *Touch me. Bear witness to these nail holes.* Outside
                the whitewashed church,
a small sign announces that Pastor Peter Hollowell will preach

                this Sunday
and that his sermon's theme will be "Keep the word of the Lord
                alway in thy mouth

for it is sweet as the honeycomb." Shall words console us?
                I try them
on my tongue. *Miasma. Wrath. Gardenia. Finch's wing. Heat lightning.*

                The silence doesn't
answer me. The turquoise-tiled baptismal pool beyond the altar is empty
                and dry, flooded

only with musty dark. God, pastor, good shepherd,
                cradle me
in your arms like a child, dip me down into the future's shadowy pool

so I may rise up
shining, so that my human flesh may evaporate with the dew
and I become

one of the congregation of roadside morning glories that last
only a few days,
that twine and climb the barbed-wire fence and make it flower.

Wind Chill

That Sunday morning, two Februaries ago, the wind chill
          made the air
feel like five below. I was walking to Emmanuel Church

          to hear the choir sing
a full Bach cantata. On the sidewalk of Boston's chic Newbury St.
          a beggar lay

on torn newspapers, huddled in a sleeping bag under a plate-glass
          store window.
Above him hovered a bald mannequin

          who wore a pearl
choker and a full-length coat of sable. Only a wealthy city
          can afford such ironies—

dark brown fur softer than silk, bed of newspapers on concrete,
          mannequin, man
separated from each other by quarter-inch-thick glass.

          It takes style. It takes
wind chill, snow driven almost straight into our faces. It takes two voices
          twining around

each other, tenor and soprano, in a passage marked "Piangevolmente,"
          meaning "weepingly."
It takes Job, naked among the ashes, flesh covered with boils, all

          his ten children
dead, to cry out and not curse God. "Remember, my life
          is but a breath

of wind. I shall never again see good days." The man
          asked me for
spare change to buy black coffee, which he would spike

          with rum.
I gave him what I had. It wasn't much. Four crumpled
          dollar bills.

Congress of Freaks with Ringling Brothers and Barnum & Bailey (Combined) Circus, Season—1929

Can there be anything
more American than this rare sepia print, a large-format-camera panorama
of the one and only

Greatest Show on Earth, shot by Edward J. Kelty, who sold
his negatives
to settle bar bills? The sword-swallower is nattily dressed in crisp-pressed

white ducks accented
with a black velour blazer and correct matching cravat. His hair's slicked back
like T.S. Eliot's,

shellacked with some pomade that smells of rum and mangoes,
which might inconceivably
be called "Night on the Nile." Has he drawn that slim three feet

of tempered Arabian
steel from his entrails like a bon mot, or is he about to swallow
it again,

a half-muttered truth whose cold thrill he feels plunge deep into
his bowels?
We'll never know, and so what? The truth is that these freaks,

the beautiful
woman who wears her floral filigree of indigo tattoos like seamless lace
hosiery or a sheer

body suit designed and "personally" sewn from gossamer
by Christian Dior,
the matron with the boa constrictor draped over

her shoulders in place
of a feather boa, even Revolvo, who stands with his back to us,
but has turned

his head around owlwise to face us with the pensive, intelligent
stare of the first
surrealists, are hard to distinguish from the two "normal" tuxedoed

ringmasters
with black butterfly bow ties. Are they Barnum and Bailey, the Ringling
            Brothers, or Tweedledum

and -dee? They stand on either end of the lineup. Tweedledee
            gazes in mock
horror and amazement at the nine-foot gentleman

            in the twenty-gallon
hat, whose red (or so I imagine it; somehow sepia suggests the actual
            colors) silk shirt

ripples like water roaring down a spillway. Both of his cowboy boots
            are stenciled in bold
white letters, TEXAS. Below him, Tom Ton, broad bottom accommodated

            by two rickety
chairs, grins back at us, rejoicing in fabulous fat, gravity's great king.
            These are mostly happy,

well-adjusted freaks. Even the snarling wild man from Borneo,
            whose huge hands
throttle the air, is only posing. My brother with Down syndrome,

            his chromosomes
a tongue twister God the stutterer couldn't get right, is as double-jointed
            as the Johnny Weissmuller

look-alike with his arms knotted in an X behind his neck.
            I remember
how Michael used to sit on our brick stoop with both legs

            curled around
his head, and how the whole neighborhood would point and marvel.
            I used to be

ashamed of him, of the way his body sometimes shook
            with an epileptic's
fury, as if he were riding a jackhammer that stammered

and tore up
the concrete beneath our feet. Michael still sways and twitches
to his nervous system's

jangled hip-hop. He cakewalks shakily down the sidewalk. He is a member
in good standing
of this congress of freaks. But aren't we all? Isn't my senile

demented father there
in the lineup, his head a dried gourd full of seeds, the maraca
an infant beats

upon the table in a tantrum? He stands by the locked unit's double doors,
punching the touch-tone
numbered buttons on a square panel, trying to break the code

that will open
sesame and release him, along with all the other forty thieves,
from their nursing home

hell. My mother, back bent from scoliosis, has the same
wrinkled, tabula rasa
face as the fortuneteller in the beaded flapper dress, this Cassandra

who foretells a future
that no one will believe until he gets there. Revolvo sees
it all, both

what's to come and what's behind him. We will
be greeted
as kin by Eko & Iko the Ambassadors from Mars, black albino twins

with dreadlocks
and crimson tunics trimmed with gold. In this anonymous lineup
everyone is wanted

by somebody for something. The cowboy giant from the great state of Texas
spreads his arms,
a wingspan of eight feet, to embrace each and every last, lost one of us.

Earth & Water

This morning I kissed my father
awake. His veined eyelids fluttered open. Now I stroke his unshaven
cheek, rough as hickory bark

and bedabbled with yolk from his poached eggs. His bloodshot left eye leaks
yellow puss. I smell
his halitosis, dark quagmire of bodily fluids, urine,

sweat, stale shit, and vomit
all mixed together, old age's slow boil. He's still in his pajamas,
dozing on his bed

at quarter to twelve. One day soon death will come, early in the morning
or late at night.
On the bedside table I see a photo of my young father celebrating

mass in a Quonset hut
for soldiers about to go into battle. There, it's Okinawa, 1945, hot.
Under his heavy chasuble

with its stitched gold cross, my father swelters. The floor of the makeshift church
is dirt. He lifts a silver
chalice toward the lips of men the same age as himself.

Stripped to the waist because
of the heat, they sweat. A few still have the lightly muscled, hairless torsos
of boys. They sip the cheap

sweet blush wine mixed with water. "The Blood of our Lord Jesus Christ,
which was shed for thee,
preserve thy body and soul. . . ." Some of these boys will die before

tomorrow's sunrise.
Everyone knows the odds. But how does Gallo sacramental rosé
at one dollar fifty cents per gallon

become Christ's blood? It is the terrible miracle of wine
turning into death,
death into birth, then back again to earth, six feet under

But it is water
I'm thinking of right now. The story my father used to tell—
before he lost his mind—

of how, just past his fifth birthday, he followed his two older brothers
and their friends to play
out on the logjam above the sawmill's dam. It was

summer, a lumber town,
Everett, Washington, 1921. Men floated the cut logs down
the river to the lake

above the dam so that they might be sawn into rough pine planks,
then seasoned in the drying
yard, in the holy fragrance of sawdust and resin. The logs spun

wetly slippery
under the boys' bare feet as they leaped their way across the lake
and shouted to each other.

They didn't notice when their friends' kid brother fell, went under
water, and didn't come
back up. It was my father's luck that the old Swede Hans Larsen,

like a shepherd with his gaff
herding the floating logs down the mill chute, saw my father's
shock of black hair

and pulled him out. Hans turned him upside down and pounded the water
from his lungs until
he took the first burning breath, opened his drowned eyes

to sunlight that stung like salt,
and heard again the mill's circular ripsaws whine and scream
through raw lumber.

Today my father reaches his trembling hand out
slowly toward the white
window sill, toward the photo of him and my mother

in a clear plexiglass
frame. "Why that's . . . that's Martha," he stammers. Mom is wearing
a red, crushed velvet

jacket and matching hat with a frilly blouse. Dad has on
a bright blue
cardigan and a gray-and-white-striped tie, which Mom has loosely

knotted around his neck.
They smile for the nursing home nurse's digital camera and flash.
"That's your sixtieth wedding

anniversary," I tell him. "How long ago was it?" he asks.
"Almost two years," I reply.
"Hard to believe," he says, gesturing vaguely toward me, my mother

in the photo, the plastic roses
unwilting on the sunlit window sill, "hard to believe all
that time's gone by."

Lord Now

        Lord now lettest thou
on Christmas day at six o' clock in the evening   *thy servant*   my father
        hooked up to his oxygen

machine   *depart*   its logo reads NewLife Lite   it whirs and hums
        then makes a sound
like coffee percolating   my father whose breathing

        is half snoring
now lettest thou   half phlegmy rattle from the fluid
        in his lungs   tail end

of the pneumonia he can't kick   the machine and he make strange
        music   the clear plastic
tube loops below his nose   its two prongs stuck into his nostrils

        to feed him air
purer than ours   *depart in peace*   he hasn't eaten in two weeks   the last
        time he drank

was three days ago   Jonathan the charge nurse checks his catheter
        bag   it's empty
"Now Reverend I'm going to clean out your mouth"   my father's

        eyes closed
to slits   Jonathan takes a white popsicle stick
        with a thimble-sized

green sponge on one end   dips it into a cup of water and swabs
        his yellow rotted teeth
lettest thou thy servant   tongue spotted white with thrush   his gray-pink

        gums   Jonathan
hums "Tender Is the Night"   puts on a latex glove and smoothes
        salve into my father's

cracked lips   another nonagenarian   Mr. Dietz with a walker
        appears in the door
"I'll be with you   in a few minutes   loverboy!"   Jonathan lifts my father

in his weightlifter's arms
resettles him   whispers "I got you Reverend"   *thy servant*
tangle of soaked sheets

thy servant depart   every two hours the nurses turn him   roll him
onto one side   and then
roll him back   a stone that has to be moved   in another two hours

they'll roll him
the other way   dying takes days   my father wears two blue
"booties"   like padded

elevator shoes   to keep his feet from getting bedsores
I read him psalms
"The dead praise not thee   O Lord   neither all they that go down in silence"

can he hear me
the oxygen tube cuts into his fat goiter-like neck   the skin
pulses   pushes out

with each breath   *depart depart*   two pairs of his scuffed black shoes
one with its laces
still knotted and tied into a bow   stand under his bureau

Mr. Dietz
stumbles down the hall with his walker   "Oh please" says a nurse
"do the Mr. Dietz shuffle

for us"   Mr. Dietz stops   a grin like a gash   flashes across
his wrinkled face
still leaning on his walker   he does a soft-shoe number in slow

motion to invisible
1920s ragtime   his slippers' leather soles
slide across

the linoleum's black and white squares   they make a soft
hush hush
depart   Fig Leaf Rag   "Time to turn the Reverend"   the nurses

hoist him up
gobs of yellow mucus and blood   a fertilized egg yolk
                broken open

drain from his mouth   "Get Jonathan!"   my father tries to cough
                can't breathe   Jonathan
aspirates the gunk from his throat   with a green squeeze-bulb attached

                to a tube   like a turkey baster
cleans his mouth with the popsicle stick and a washcloth   gives him
                another shot of morphine

the nurses change the sheets and pillowcases   his breathing grows shallow
                stops for several seconds
starts abruptly   I put my hand on his chest   wet breath

                rumbles in his lungs
it's like putting one's hand on the handle of a pot of water
                under a burner turned

to high   feeling the water   start to simmer   then boil
                depart in peace
it goes on   me stroking his hot liver-spotted

                forehead   that chapped skin
holding his hand turned   cyanotic blue   "O God
                thou hast cast us out

and scattered us abroad"   big knuckles and ridges of bone
                tendons sticking up
through old skin   "And as a vesture shalt thou

                change them
and they shall be changed"   I touch breastbone   ribs arms feet kneecaps
                ears nose wrinkled

waxy cheek and neck   trying to hold him here
                peace peace peace
he my father   unconscious   lifts one eyebrow   as if to say

> he hears me
peace   *depart in peace*   he keeps breathing   like a croupy infant
> the evening nurses leave

night shift comes on   from the small Greek icon
> above my father's bureau
Christ looks down   eyes black   pupilless   two holes bored

> into a pine plank
Lord now   a nurse down the hall turns on the radio   staticky
> Christmas carols

"We three kings of Orient are   Bearing gifts we traverse
> afar"   a crumpled
brown paper towel on his metal rolling table   *lettest thou*   *now*

Looking for My Father in Aix-en-Provence, Early March

I.

I look for my father in the open-air flea market along the Cours Mirabeau, where they
        sell raw silk scarves of all colors and straw baskets of all shapes and sizes

*

I finger the silk, let it slide across the back of my hand to feel its nubbly smoothness

*

I imagine carrying home a dozen brown eggs, russet potatoes, and leeks in a new
        shopping basket with one cane dyed red, woven in and out among the white
        undyed canes like a ribbon running around its circumference

*

I look and look but buy nothing

*

I do not find him at the fountain where the naked stone boys ride dolphins that jet
        water from their mouths

*

They turn the fountains off after midnight

*

I look for him at the all-night boulangerie where I buy a crusted baguette "de la
        festivale" with pointed ends and afterwards walk the dark narrow cobbled
        streets, eating as I go

*

I do not find him, my ghostly boulevardier in his white-on-white pinstriped suit,
        strolling with the crowd along the Avenue Victor Hugo, which changes its

name to the Boulevard du Roi René, then to the Boulevard Carnot, to the
    Cours Saint-Louis, to the Boulevard Aristide Briand, to the Cours Sextius,
    to the Avenue Napoléon Bonaparte before becoming the Avenue Victor
    Hugo again

*

He does not linger over and savor the truite amandine at the table next to the door at
    the Brasserie Carillon

*

He does not flake its flesh from the small bones with his fork

*

He is fog clinging like lamb's wool to the steep terraced hillsides early in the morning

*

No, he is the smoke from the brush fires that farmers tend with metal rakes as they
    burn off their land

*

No

*

He is neither of these

*

He is not among the cypresses that stand like dark torches on either side of the gate
    next to the snarling sandstone lions

*

I look for him among the rows of pollarded plane trees that line the streets and
    throw their late-afternoon shadows on the cream-, gray-, or orange-tinged
    limestone walls of 15th-century houses

Their shadows are those of upraised hands with fingers outstretched, beseeching
      blessing

*

I look for my father's sermons among the spray-painted black and pastel hieroglyphs
      of graffiti on the ancient stone walls

*

I find only "Antoinette, On T'Aime"

*

Antoinette, whom everybody loves

*

I look for him at the salon de thé, where a pregnant woman drinks black tea from Sri
      Lanka, which tastes like smoke from burning eucalyptus branches, and dips
      almond macaroons into her cup

*

While she drinks, she gives suck to her first, year-old child who guzzles and slurps
      the thin sweet milk from her white, blue-veined, globed left breast

*

Her husband with the three-day beard is slim, beautiful, and attentive

*

He bends across the table toward her

*

What do they say to each other

*

They are so young

*

How will they live their lives

*

I look for my father on the "Impasse Fleurie," which translates as "enflowered
cul-de-sac"

*

Only the pear trees are blossoming, levitating in the backyards of houses with red tile
roofs

*

They float there like cast-off bridal veils

*

The one stout palm tree's fronds rustle in the wind

*

I could say that the mistral roughs up my hair like a father running thick clumsy
fingers through his son's hair, but I would be wrong

*

The mistral through the cypresses makes the sound of surf on a white beach three
thousand miles away

II.

I look for my father behind the red double doors of Cézanne's studio on the hill at
    Les Lauves

*

The red paint is flaking

*

The brass handles have been polished to the dull luster of lake water at dawn by one
    hundred and five years of hands opening and shutting those doors

*

Inside I find only three skulls on a gray chest of drawers

*

Three green bottles, one of turpentine, one of linseed oil, and one half-full of red
    wine, the vin ordinaire

*

The rotting fruit Cézanne loved to paint in his still lives—shriveled apples, pears,
    lemons

*

A bowl of small yellow onions, which have sloughed off their dry papery skins

*

I've always loved how "still life" translates into French as "nature morte"

*

My father is the one streak of royal blue among the smeared greens, yellows, reds,
ochers, and grays on Cézanne's rectangular palette

*

The thin pine palette has warped, gone wavy

*

Its one thumbhole is a Cyclops' blind eye off-center

*

All that's left of Cézanne in this room is one pencil drawing of a skull and four half-
finished watercolors—one of a vase of irises, another of a row of eight
large flowerpots with shrubs growing from them, another of a white plaster
Cupid without arms, and one of a river with thirteen naked male bathers

*

Next to the watercolor Cupid stands the plaster cast

*

Neither is more real than the other

*

All that's left of Cézanne is a black cap with a visor, his black bowler, his everyday
olive overcoat, his black wool Sunday coat, and two umbrellas hanging on
pegs by the door, waiting for him to go out

*

He will not return

*

It is not raining today

All that's left of Cézanne is his olive work smock flecked with blue, white, and gray
  paint

The only thing that lasts is sunlight flooding through the thirty large panes of glass
  that form the studio's northern wall

The long shadows we cast near dusk, our short shadows at noon

Elegy with Lord Shiva & Peonies

I.

Father, patron saint of Alzheimer's, show me
how to lose the world, noun by noun, leaf by stone, herons

by Easter eggs by red tulips opening
in a cut-glass bowl that throws its broken rain-

bows around the room when the sun streams through our
skylight. To lose each infinite infinitive,

radiant imperative—to perambulate,
siphon, hoard, haggle, loosen, listen, snooze, lust,

genuflect. And then the liminal lusters
of tenses—the imperfect, pluperfect, past

conditional, subjunctive. *She was speaking,*
he had had too much borscht, we would have given

the car keys to you, if he were mine. Father,
patron saint of syntax tangled as briars,

pull the world up by its word roots and stammer—
son, sonagram, sonar, sonata, sooey,

sunny—without ever uttering the one word
I want. Scramble all our prepositions of

time and place. Stumble on through *beyond before*
to *after within.* Go past *behind during.*

Help me too to lose *a* door, *the* backhoe,
an apple—exactitudes of definite

and indefinite articles—and remain
unmoved. Father, patron saint of the void, O,

ovoid, black hole into which our lives get crammed,
I shall finally relinquish the pronouns.

There will be no one to pencil these words
on unlined sheets of paper, which I must keep

erasing. Father, Alzheimer's has its own
intractable grammar. Even if you were

alive, you would not be able to tell me
what day it is. Father, if I could call you

again on the telephone, I would tell you
today is Wednesday, the seventeenth of May.

II.

Today is Wednesday, the seventeenth of May.
My neighbor's peonies have begun to bloom.

Buds the size of hard, black rubber "super balls"
open frilled white petals, cut from the same sheer

silk as my wife's cream chemise. At our younger
daughter's elementary school, every Wednesday

is show and tell. A child brings in a monarch
butterfly in a small cage of chicken wire.

She explains the life cycle of monarchs and
then releases the butterfly from its cage

so it too can migrate, lay, and die. Its wings
open and close like a rusted hinge escaped

from its doorframe. The kids clap. Father, you too
were once seven years old. The world expanded

and proliferated around you, a world
that would contract in your last years to one room

with one window, through which the sun mapped your north
wall with light and leaf shadows. The children bring

cutworm caterpillars, black lace mantillas
from Barcelona, airplanes with balsa wings,

an Amish great-grandmother's Center Diamond
quilt, whose greens, blues, and purples glow, mesmerize

the eye like Frank Stella's color-field paintings,
a telephone of steel wire stretched taut between

two tin cans, fiddlehead ferns which one can sauté
and eat with soy sauce and lemon juice, a stag's

seven-pronged antlers like a candelabra,
an iPod downloaded with all of Mozart's

symphonies, fossilized trilobites, geodes,
a statuette of four-armed Shiva dancing

within a circle of fire. The god's upper
right hand holds a drum shaped like an hourglass.

III.

When Shiva beats his helter-skelter rhythms
from the dried skin stretched tight across the hollow

drum, the world comes into being. His upper
left hand holds the flames that will destroy this world.

He raises his lower right hand's copper palm
to bless and protect us. His lower left palm

extends downward, held out empty and flat, sign
of surrender. The heels of his lower palms

almost touch, so it seems his hands are clapping
out the beat of the dance. Our Lord Shiva lifts

his left leg high to the right until it's nearly
horizontal, signifying the soul's

liberation from maya, our sensory
realm's seven torn veils of illusion. Shiva's

right foot tramples a screaming prostrate infant.
Father, remember how peaceful you became

when memory first deserted you? You sat
for hours on the sagging couch that leaked

cotton batting, held hands with Michael, my brother
who has Down syndrome. My mother groaned, "Now I

have two idiots to care for!" Two rag dolls,
heads stuffed with sawdust. My art book says the god's

flexed foot pressing the child down into the dirt
is a symbol of "forgetfulness and, thus, grace."

IV.

Father, patron saint of dirt, we live between
the two injunctions *remember* and *forget*.

Because you have forgotten your life and all
that it held, I would tell it to you again.

Let's start with the peonies. Some are fragrant,
some aren't. Red, lavender, white, rose, cream—inhale

each. Jim W. at the Heartland Peony
Society's website says, "Fragrance can be

different in the morning than in the evening
and some varieties are fragrant for all

their open-time while others are just passingly
fragrant." It is impossible to describe

their smell. One Zen master's koan to whack
his disciples onward toward enlightenment

was "Describe the taste of the umeboshi
plum!" The correct answer will always be

to shrug, guffaw like an idiot, then grin.

V.

The ones called "Snow Mountain" in my neighbor's
backyard! To smell them is to hold a full

crystal wineglass of chilled pinot grigio
to one's nostrils, to inhale that sweet tartness

and never be able to drink it. I will
never be enlightened by lightning strike

laughter. I love words too much, the big vulgar
peonies. There are over four hundred hybrids!

To say their names is to recite the entire
history of what it means to live: *Birthday,*

Do Tell, Kamikaze, Kansas, Raspberry
Ice, Red Charm, Truly Yours, Apache, Ave

Maria, Col. McCormack, Glory
Hallelujah, Mother's Day, Flanders Fields,

Fortune Teller, Rapture, Requiem, Dolorodell,
Elsa Sass, Cleopatra. Father, forget

the names. They are not all we have. For now
bow your head to the white peonies starting

to open with 14-karat gold anthers
at their centers. See how black ants swarm over

and into the split green buds. They want nectar.
They bore into the sweet core. Some say the ants

help the buds to blossom, loosen the outer
sheaf so the super balls spring, bounce, burst forth, birth

huge double flowers. Each moment sustains and
devours. Remember to forget, forget to

remember. Father, patron saint of black ants,
already the petals wilt, brown, and litter

the dew-drenched mulch. What shredded kleenex! Bless all
rot. Teach me topsoil, clay, gravel, water table,

runoff. Come back as the hollow silver maple's
roots that still grow, clutch, crack our sidewalk.

Acknowledgments

The author gratefully thanks the editors of the following publications in which these poems, sometimes in slightly different versions, first appeared:

Alaska Quarterly Review: "Looking for My Father in Aix-en-Provence, Early March"

Antioch Review: "Spring Does Covers & Original Numbers"

Black Warrior Review: "End Game"

BOMB: "Elegy in the Rainbow Season," "Grout," "My Brother's Mirror"

Chelsea: "First Frost," "Mid-March at the Park, 2003"

Crab Orchard Review: "Provider"

Epoch: "After the Death of the Poet"

Flying Island: "En Passant"

Green Mountains Review: "Earth & Water," "Wind Chill"

Michigan Quarterly Review: "Girls with Glow-in-the-Dark Hula Hoops"

Notre Dame Review: "Consolation Baptist Church," "Loose Change & Molars"

Passages North: "Sentence Fragment Ending in Sleep's Ellipsis," "The Breakage"

Poetry Northwest: "Child Sleeping"

Prairie Schooner: "Elegy in Spring Snow"

Quarterly West: "Spring Theophanies," "Winter Water"

Southern Review: "Bloodstone," "Congress of Freaks with Ringling Brothers and Barnum & Bailey (Combined) Circus, Season—1929," "Dirt Angels"

Sou'wester: "Elegy with Lord Shiva & Peonies"

Third Coast: "Lord Now," "What Form Shall the Soul Take?"

Virginia Quarterly Review: "Forsythia"

William and Mary Review: "Human Poem," "Jumping the Waves."

Thanks to the Virginia Center for the Creative Arts and the Ragdale Foundation for residencies and to Purdue University for a Center for Creative Endeavors Fellowship, all of which were essential to the writing of these poems. Thanks to William Olsen for selecting this book for publication in the Green Rose Poetry Series and for his careful editing. The author is profoundly grateful to Bruce Beasley, Daniel Corrie, Mary Leader, Daniel Morris, and Dana Roeser for their comments on drafts of these poems and on the book manuscript. As always, he is indebted to his family—Dana Roeser, Eleanor and Lucy Platt, and Martha and Michael Platt—for their love and support.

photo by Lucy Platt

Donald Platt is a professor of English at Purdue University. His first two collections, *Fresh Peaches, Fireworks, & Guns* and *Cloud Atlas*, were published by Purdue University Press as winners of the Verna Emery Poetry Prize. His third book, *My Father Says Grace*, was published by the University of Arkansas Press. He is a recipient of the "Discovery"/*The Nation* Prize, a fellowship from the National Endowment for the Arts, the Center for Book Arts' Poetry Chapbook Prize, and two Pushcart Prizes. His poems have appeared in many magazines and journals, including *The New Republic, Nation, Paris Review, Poetry, Kenyon Review, Georgia Review, Virginia Quarterly Review, Field, Iowa Review, Southwest Review,* and *Southern Review,* and have been anthologized in *The Best American Poetry* 2000 and 2006. He lives with his wife, the poet Dana Roeser, and their two daughters in West Lafayette, Indiana.

New Issues Poetry

Lance Larsen, *Erasable Walls*
David Dodd Lee, *Abrupt Rural; Downsides of Fish Culture*
M.L. Liebler, *The Moon a Box*
Alexander Long, *Vigil*
Deanne Lundin, *The Ginseng Hunter's Notebook*
Barbara Maloutas, *In a Combination of Practices*
Joy Manesiotis, *They Sing to Her Bones*
Sarah Mangold, *Household Mechanics*
Gail Martin, *The Hourglass Heart*
Justin Marks, *A Million in Prizes*
David Marlatt, *A Hog Slaughtering Woman*
Louise Mathias, *Lark Apprentice*
Gretchen Mattox, *Buddha Box; Goodnight Architecture*
Carrie McGath, *Small Murders*
Paula McLain, *Less of Her; Stumble, Gorgeous*
Lydia Melvin, *South of Here*
Sarah Messer, *Bandit Letters*
Wayne Miller, *Only the Senses Sleep*
Malena Mörling, *Ocean Avenue*
Julie Moulds, *The Woman with a Cubed Head*
Carsten René Nielsen, *The World Cut Out with Crooked Scissors*
Marsha de la O, *Black Hope*
C. Mikal Oness, *Water Becomes Bone*
Bradley Paul, *The Obvious*
Jennifer Perrine, *The Body Is No Machine*
Katie Peterson, *This One Tree*
Jon Pineda, *The Translator's Diary*
Donald Platt, *Dirt Angels*
Elizabeth Powell, *The Republic of Self*
Margaret Rabb, *Granite Dives*
Rebecca Reynolds, *Daughter of the Hangnail; The Bovine Two-Step*
Martha Rhodes, *Perfect Disappearance*
Beth Roberts, *Brief Moral History in Blue*
John Rybicki, *Traveling at High Speeds* (expanded 2nd edition)
Mary Ann Samyn, *Inside the Yellow Dress; Purr*
Ever Saskya, *The Porch is a Journey Different from the House*
Mark Scott, *Tactile Values*
Hugh Seidman, *Somebody Stand Up and Sing*
Heather Sellers, *The Boys I Borrow*
Martha Serpas, *Côte Blanche*
Diane Seuss-Brakeman, *It Blows You Hollow*
Elaine Sexton, *Sleuth; Causeway*
Patty Seyburn, *Hilarity*
Marc Sheehan, *Greatest Hits*

Heidi Lynn Staples, *Guess Can Gallop*
Phillip Sterling, *Mutual Shores*
Angela Sorby, *Distance Learning*
Matthew Thorburn, *Subject to Change*
Russell Thorburn, *Approximate Desire*
Rodney Torreson, *A Breathable Light*
Lee Upton, *Undid in the Land of Undone*
Robert VanderMolen, *Breath*
Martin Walls, *Small Human Detail in Care of National Trust*
Patricia Jabbeh Wesley, *Before the Palm Could Bloom: Poems of Africa*